The Eclectic Literary Club

Vol. IX

George Washington's
Rules of Civility & Decent Behaviour
in Company and Conversation

Compliments of

GREENPORT
FINANCIAL ADVISERS INC.®

Est. 1989

"Reading is to the mind what exercise is to the body."

Joseph Addison
1672-1719

A.D. 2009

George Washington's Rules *of* Civility & Decent Behaviour *in* Company *and* Conversation

Engraving of George Washington from Jesse Ames Spencer's
History of the United States

George Washington's

Rules *of* Civility &

Decent Behaviour

in Company *and*

Conversation

CICO BOOKS

LONDON NEW YORK

First published in 2007 by Cico Books

an imprint of Ryland, Peters & Small Ltd

519 Broadway, 5th Floor, New York, NY 10012

10 9 8 7 6 5 4 3 2 1

CIP catalog record for this book is available from the Library of Congress

ISBN-10: 1 904991 74 2

ISBN-13: 978 1 904991 74 8

Printed in China

Editor: Alison Wormleighton

Designer: Roger Hammond

PREFACE

Today, when most of us at times long for more civilized behavior from those around us, this little book of advice about civility could not be more relevant. Although some of its maxims are amusingly quaint and endearingly old-fashioned, most are as applicable today as when they were written – which is astonishing, since these "rules" are thought to have come from books published in Europe and used by polite society from the late 1500s onward. Moreover, those books were probably based upon classical sources such as Aristotle and Cicero, as well as medieval codes of chivalry and Renaissance "courtesy books."

By the mid-1700s, 110 of these precepts were being diligently copied down by the 14- or 15-year-old George Washington, probably during school lectures. A serious, industrious, self-sufficient boy, he would have taken to heart the principles of self-discipline, dignified behavior and consideration for others underlying these precepts. Indeed, they are qualities for which he later became widely known, and historians believe that these maxims had a formative influence on the boy who was to become the "father of his country." As you can see from this volume of *George Washington's Rules of Civility and Decent Behaviour*, what constitutes civilized behavior never really changes.

· 1st ·

Every Action done in Company ought to be with Some Sign of Respect to those that are Present.

· 2nd ·

When in Company, put not your Hands to any Part of the Body, not usually Discovered.

· 3rd ·

Shew Nothing to your Friend that may affright him.

· 4th ·

*I*N THE PRESENCE OF

OTHERS SING NOT TO YOURSELF

WITH A HUMMING NOISE,

NOR DRUM WITH YOUR FINGERS

OR FEET.

· 5th ·

If You Cough, Sneeze, Sigh,
or Yawn, do it not Loud but
Privately; and Speak not in your
Yawning, but put Your
Handkerchief or Hand before your
face and turn aside.

· 6th ·

Sleep not when others Speak,
Sit not when others stand,
Speak not when you Should hold
your Peace, walk not on
when others Stop.

· 7th ·

PUT NOT OFF YOUR CLOTHES
IN THE PRESENCE OF OTHERS, NOR
GO OUT YOUR CHAMBER
HALF DRESSED.

· 8th ·

AT PLAY AND AT FIRE
IT'S GOOD MANNERS TO GIVE PLACE
TO THE LAST COMER, AND
AFFECT NOT TO SPEAK LOUDER
THAN ORDINARY.

· 9th ·

SPIT NOT IN THE FIRE,
nor STOOP LOW BEFORE IT, NEITHER
PUT YOUR HANDS INTO THE
FLAMES TO WARM THEM, NOR SET
YOUR FEET UPON THE FIRE
ESPECIALLY IF THERE BE
MEAT BEFORE IT.

· 10th ·

WHEN YOU SIT DOWN,
KEEP YOUR FEET FIRM AND EVEN,
WITHOUT PUTTING ONE ON THE OTHER
OR CROSSING THEM.

· 11th ·

SHIFT NOT YOURSELF IN THE
SIGHT OF OTHERS NOR GNAW
YOUR NAILS.

Shake not the head, Feet, or

Legs. Roll not the Eyes, lift not one

eyebrow higher than the other,

wry not the mouth, and bedew no

man's face with your Spittle,

by approaching too near him

when you Speak.

*K*ILL NO VERMIN AS FLEAS, LICE, TICKS &c

IN THE SIGHT OF OTHERS. IF YOU SEE ANY FILTH OR THICK

SPITTLE, PUT YOUR FOOT DEXTROUSLY UPON IT;

IF IT BE UPON THE CLOTHES OF YOUR COMPANIONS,

PUT IT OFF PRIVATELY, AND IF IT BE UPON

YOUR OWN CLOTHES, RETURN THANKS TO

HIM WHO PUTS IT OFF.

· 14th ·

Turn not your Back
to others, especially in Speaking.
Jog not the Table or Desk
on which Another reads or writes.
Lean not upon anyone.

· 15th ·

Keep your Nails clean and
Short, also your Hands and Teeth
Clean, yet without Shewing
any great Concern
for them.

· 16th ·

Do not Puff up the Cheeks,
Loll not out the tongue, rub the Hands,
or beard, thrust out the lips, or
bite them or keep the Lips too open
or too Close.

· 17th ·

Be no Flatterer, neither Play with
any that delights not to be
Played Withal.

· 18th ·

READ NO LETTERS, BOOKS, OR
PAPERS IN COMPANY BUT WHEN
THERE IS A NECESSITY FOR THE DOING
OF IT YOU MUST ASK LEAVE:
COME NOT NEAR THE BOOKS OR
WRITINGS OF ANOTHER SO AS
TO READ THEM UNLESS
DESIRED OR GIVE YOUR OPINION OF
THEM UNASKED, ALSO LOOK
NOT NIGH WHEN ANOTHER
IS WRITING A LETTER.

· 19th ·

LET YOUR COUNTENANCE BE PLEASANT BUT IN
SERIOUS MATTERS SOMEWHAT GRAVE.

· 20th ·

THE GESTURES OF THE BODY MUST BE SUITED TO THE
DISCOURSE YOU ARE UPON.

· 21st ·

REPROACH NONE FOR THE INFIRMITIES
OF NATURE, NOR DELIGHT TO PUT THEM THAT HAVE
IN MIND THEREOF.

· 22nd ·

SHEW NOT YOURSELF GLAD AT THE MISFORTUNE OF
ANOTHER THOUGH HE WERE YOUR ENEMY.

· 23rd ·

WHEN YOU SEE A CRIME PUNISHED, YOU MAY BE
INWARDLY PLEASED; BUT ALWAYS SHEW PITY TO THE
SUFFERING OFFENDER.

· 24th ·

DO NOT LAUGH TOO LOUD OR TOO MUCH AT ANY
PUBLIC SPECTACLE.

· 25th ·

SUPERFLUOUS COMPLIMENTS AND ALL
AFFECTATION OF CEREMONY ARE TO BE AVOIDED,
YET WHERE DUE THEY ARE NOT
TO BE NEGLECTED.

· 26th ·

IN PULLING OFF YOUR HAT TO PERSONS OF
DISTINCTION, AS NOBLEMEN, JUSTICES, CHURCHMEN
&C MAKE A REVERENCE, BOWING MORE OR
LESS ACCORDING TO THE CUSTOM OF THE
BETTER BRED, AND QUALITY OF THE PERSON.
AMONGST YOUR EQUALS EXPECT NOT
ALWAYS THAT THEY SHOULD BEGIN WITH
YOU FIRST, BUT TO PULL OFF THE HAT WHEN
THERE IS NO NEED IS AFFECTATION. IN THE
MANNER OF SALUTING AND RESALUTING IN
WORDS, KEEP TO THE MOST
USUAL CUSTOM.

· 27TH ·

'TIS ILL MANNERS TO BID ONE MORE EMINENT

THAN YOURSELF BE COVERED AS WELL AS NOT TO DO IT TO

WHOM IT'S DUE. LIKEWISE HE THAT MAKES

TOO MUCH HASTE TO PUT ON HIS HAT DOES NOT WELL,

YET HE OUGHT TO PUT IT ON AT THE FIRST, OR

AT MOST THE SECOND TIME OF BEING ASKED; NOW WHAT IS

HEREIN SPOKEN, OF QUALIFICATION IN

BEHAVIOUR IN SALUTING, OUGHT ALSO TO BE OBSERVED

IN TAKING OF PLACE, AND SITTING

DOWN FOR CEREMONIES WITHOUT BOUNDS

IS TROUBLESOME.

IF ANYONE COME TO SPEAK TO YOU
WHILE YOU ARE SITTING, STAND UP THOUGH
HE BE YOUR INFERIOR, AND WHEN YOU
PRESENT SEATS LET IT BE TO
EVERYONE ACCORDING TO
HIS DEGREE.

· 29th ·

WHEN YOU MEET WITH ONE OF
GREATER QUALITY THAN YOURSELF, STOP,
AND RETIRE ESPECIALLY IF IT BE AT
A DOOR OR ANY STRAIGHT PLACE TO GIVE
WAY FOR HIM TO PASS.

· 30th ·

IN WALKING, THE HIGHEST PLACE IN
MOST COUNTRIES SEEMS TO BE ON THE RIGHT
HAND THEREFORE PLACE YOURSELF ON
THE LEFT OF HIM WHOM YOU DESIRE TO
HONOUR: BUT IF THREE WALK TOGETHER THE
MIDDEST PLACE IS THE MOST HONOURABLE;
THE WALL IS USUALLY GIVEN TO THE
MOST WORTHY IF TWO WALK
TOGETHER.

· 31st ·

IF ANYONE FAR SURPASSES OTHERS,
EITHER IN AGE, ESTATE, OR MERIT YET WOULD
GIVE PLACE TO A MEANER THAN HIMSELF
IN HIS OWN LODGING OR ELSEWHERE, THE ONE
OUGHT NOT TO ACCEPT IT, SO HE ON THE
OTHER PART SHOULD NOT USE MUCH
EARNESTNESS NOR OFFER IT ABOVE
ONCE OR TWICE.

TO ONE THAT IS EQUAL, OR NOT MUCH

INFERIOR, YOU ARE TO GIVE CHIEF PLACE

IN YOUR LODGING AND HE TO WHO 'TIS

OFFERED OUGHT AT THE FIRST TO REFUSE

IT BUT AT THE SECOND TO ACCEPT

THOUGH NOT WITHOUT ACKNOWLEDGING

HIS OWN UNWORTHINESS.

·33rd·

They that are in Dignity or in office have in all places Precedency but whilst they are Young they ought to respect those that are their equals in Birth or other Qualities, though they have no Public charge.

· 34th ·

It is good Manners to prefer them to whom we Speak before ourselves, especially if they be above us with whom in no Sort we ought to begin.

· 35th ·

Let your Discourse with Men of Business be Short and Comprehensive.

· 36th ·

ARTIFICERS & PERSONS OF
LOW DEGREE OUGHT NOT TO USE MANY
CEREMONIES TO LORDS, OR OTHERS OF
HIGH DEGREE BUT RESPECT AND HIGHLY
HONOUR THEM, AND THOSE OF
HIGH DEGREE OUGHT TO TREAT THEM
WITH AFFABILITY & COURTESY,
WITHOUT ARROGANCY.

· 37th ·

IN SPEAKING TO MEN OF
QUALITY DO NOT LEAN NOR LOOK
THEM FULL IN THE FACE, NOR APPROACH
TOO NEAR THEM. AT LEAST KEEP A FULL
PACE FROM THEM.

· 38th ·

IN VISITING THE SICK, DO NOT
PRESENTLY PLAY THE PHYSICIAN IF YOU
BE NOT KNOWING THEREIN.

· 39th ·

IN WRITING OR SPEAKING,
GIVE TO EVERY PERSON HIS DUE TITLE
ACCORDING TO HIS DEGREE & THE
CUSTOM OF THE PLACE.

· 40th ·

STRIVE NOT WITH YOUR SUPERIORS IN
ARGUMENT, BUT ALWAYS SUBMIT YOUR JUDGMENT TO
OTHERS WITH MODESTY.

· 41st ·

UNDERTAKE NOT TO TEACH YOUR EQUAL
IN THE ART HIMSELF PROFESSES; IT SAVOURS
OF ARROGANCY.

· 42nd ·

LET THY CEREMONIES IN COURTESY BE
PROPER TO THE DIGNITY OF HIS PLACE WITH WHOM
THOU CONVERSES, FOR IT IS ABSURD TO ACT
THE SAME WITH A CLOWN AND A PRINCE.

· 43rd ·

*D*o not express joy

before one sick or in pain

for that contrary Passion

will aggravate his

Misery.

WHEN A MAN DOES ALL HE CAN
THOUGH IT SUCCEEDS NOT WELL BLAME NOT
HIM THAT DID IT.

BEING TO ADVISE OR REPREHEND
ANYONE, CONSIDER WHETHER IT OUGHT TO BE
IN PUBLIC OR IN PRIVATE; PRESENTLY,
OR AT SOME OTHER TIME, IN WHAT
TERMS TO DO IT & IN REPROVING SHEW NO
SIGN OF CHOLER BUT DO IT WITH ALL
SWEETNESS AND MILDNESS.

· 46th ·

TAKE ALL ADMONITIONS THANKFULLY
IN WHAT TIME OR PLACE 'SOEVER GIVEN BUT
AFTERWARDS NOT BEING CULPABLE TAKE
A TIME & PLACE CONVENIENT TO
LET HIM KNOW IT THAT
GAVE THEM.

· 47th ·

MOCK NOT NOR JEST AT ANYTHING
OF IMPORTANCE; BREAK NO JEST THAT ARE
SHARP BITING AND IF YOU DELIVER
ANYTHING WITTY AND PLEASANT,
ABSTAIN FROM LAUGHING
THEREAT YOURSELF.

· 48th ·

Wherein you reprove

Another, be unblameable yourself;

for example is more prevalent

than Precepts.

· 49th ·

Use no Reproachful Language against anyone neither Curse nor Revile.

· 50th ·

Be not hasty to believe flying Reports to the Disparagement of any.

· 51st ·

Wear not your Clothes, foul, unripped, or Dusty but See they be Brushed once every day at least and take heed that you approach not to any uncleanness.

*I*N YOUR APPAREL BE

MODEST AND ENDEAVOUR TO

ACCOMMODATE NATURE, RATHER THAN

TO PROCURE ADMIRATION; KEEP TO

THE FASHION OF YOUR EQUALS

SUCH AS ARE CIVIL AND

ORDERLY WITH RESPECT TO TIMES

AND PLACES.

· 53rd ·

Run not in the Streets, neither go
too slowly nor with Mouth open. Go not
Shaking your Arms, kick not the earth
with your feet, go not upon the Toes,
nor in a Dancing fashion.

· 54th ·

Play not the Peacock, looking everywhere
about you, to See if you be well Decked, if your
Shoes fit well, if your Stockings Sit
neatly, and Clothes handsomely.

· 55th ·

Eat not in the Streets, nor in the House,
out of Season.

ASSOCIATE YOURSELF WITH MEN OF GOOD QUALITY
IF YOU ESTEEM YOUR OWN REPUTATION; FOR
'TIS BETTER TO BE ALONE THAN IN
BAD COMPANY.

IN WALKING UP AND DOWN IN A HOUSE,
ONLY WITH ONE IN COMPANY, IF HE BE GREATER THAN
YOURSELF, AT THE FIRST GIVE HIM THE RIGHT HAND
AND STOP NOT TILL HE DOES AND BE NOT
THE FIRST THAT TURNS, AND WHEN YOU DO TURN LET
IT BE WITH YOUR FACE TOWARDS HIM; IF
HE BE A MAN OF GREAT QUALITY, WALK NOT WITH HIM
CHEEK BY JOWL BUT SOMEWHAT BEHIND HIM;
BUT YET IN SUCH A MANNER THAT HE
MAY EASILY SPEAK TO YOU.

*L*ET YOUR CONVERSATION

BE WITHOUT MALICE OR ENVY,

FOR 'TIS A SIGN OF A

TRACTABLE AND COMMENDABLE

NATURE; AND IN ALL CAUSES

OF PASSION ADMIT REASON

TO GOVERN.

· 59th ·

Never express anything

unbecoming, nor Act against

the Rules Moral before

your inferiors.

· 60th ·

BE NOT IMMODEST IN URGING YOUR
FRIENDS TO DISCOVER A SECRET.

· 61st ·

UTTER NOT BASE AND
FRIVOLOUS THINGS AMONGST GRAVE
AND LEARNED MEN NOR VERY
DIFFICULT QUESTIONS OR SUBJECTS
AMONG THE IGNORANT, OR
THINGS HARD TO BE BELIEVED; STUFF
NOT YOUR DISCOURSE WITH
SENTENCES AMONGST YOUR BETTERS
NOR EQUALS.

· 62nd ·

Speak not of doleful Things in a
Time of Mirth or at the Table; Speak not of
Melancholy Things as Death and Wounds, and if
others Mention them Change if you can
the Discourse; tell not your Dreams,
but to your intimate Friend.

· 63rd ·

A Man ought not to value himself of his
Achievements, or rare Qualities of wit; much
less of his riches, Virtue or Kindred.

· 64th ·

BREAK NOT A JEST WHERE NONE
TAKE PLEASURE IN MIRTH. LAUGH NOT ALOUD, NOR
AT ALL WITHOUT OCCASION; DERIDE NO
MAN'S MISFORTUNE, THOUGH THERE SEEM
TO BE SOME CAUSE.

· 65th ·

SPEAK NOT INJURIOUS WORDS
NEITHER IN JEST NOR EARNEST. SCOFF AT NONE
ALTHOUGH THEY GIVE OCCASION.

Be not forward but friendly
and Courteous; the first to
Salute, hear and answer; & be
not Pensive when it's a time to
Converse.

· 67th ·

Detract not from others; neither
be excessive in Commanding.

· 68th ·

Go not thither, where
you know not, whether you Shall
be Welcome or not. Give not Advice
without being asked & when
desired do it briefly.

· 69th ·

If two contend together take not
the part of either unconstrained;
and be not obstinate in your own
Opinion, in Things indifferent be of
the Major Side.

· 70th ·

Reprehend not the imperfections of
others for that belongs to Parents,
Masters, and Superiors.

GAZE NOT ON THE MARKS

OR BLEMISHES OF OTHERS AND

ASK NOT HOW THEY CAME. WHAT

YOU MAY SPEAK IN SECRET TO

YOUR FRIEND DELIVER NOT

BEFORE OTHERS.

SPEAK NOT IN AN UNKNOWN TONGUE IN COMPANY
BUT IN YOUR OWN LANGUAGE AND THAT AS THOSE OF
QUALITY DO AND NOT AS THE VULGAR; SUBLIME
MATTERS TREAT SERIOUSLY.

THINK BEFORE YOU SPEAK, PRONOUNCE NOT
IMPERFECTLY NOR BRING OUT YOUR WORDS TOO HASTILY
BUT ORDERLY & DISTINCTLY.

WHEN ANOTHER SPEAKS, BE ATTENTIVE YOURSELF
AND DISTURB NOT THE AUDIENCE. IF ANY HESITATE IN HIS
WORDS, HELP HIM NOT, NOR PROMPT HIM WITHOUT
DESIRED, INTERRUPT HIM NOT, NOR ANSWER HIM
TILL HIS SPEECH BE ENDED.

· 75th ·

IN THE MIDST OF DISCOURSE ASK NOT OF WHAT ONE
TREATETH, BUT IF YOU PERCEIVE ANY STOP BECAUSE OF
YOUR COMING, YOU MAY WELL ENTREAT HIM GENTLY TO
PROCEED: IF A PERSON OF QUALITY COMES IN WHILE YOU'RE
CONVERSING IT'S HANDSOME TO REPEAT WHAT
WAS SAID BEFORE.

*W*HILE YOU ARE TALKING,

POINT NOT WITH YOUR FINGER

AT HIM OF WHOM YOU DISCOURSE

NOR APPROACH TOO NEAR HIM

TO WHOM YOU TALK,

ESPECIALLY TO HIS FACE.

· 77th ·

Treat with men at fit Times about
Business & Whisper not in the Company
of Others.

· 78th ·

Make no Comparisons and if any
of the Company be Commended for any
brave act of Virtue, commend not
another for the Same.

· 79th ·

Be not apt to relate News if
you know not the truth thereof.
In Discoursing of things you Have heard,
Name not your Author always. A Secret
Discover not.

· 80th ·

BE NOT TEDIOUS IN DISCOURSE OR
IN READING UNLESS YOU FIND THE
COMPANY PLEASED THEREWITH.

· 81st ·

BE NOT CURIOUS TO KNOW THE
AFFAIRS OF OTHERS, NEITHER
APPROACH THOSE THAT
SPEAK IN PRIVATE.

· 82nd ·

UNDERTAKE NOT WHAT YOU CANNOT
PERFORM, BUT BE CAREFUL TO KEEP
YOUR PROMISE.

· 83rd ·

*W*HEN YOU DELIVER A

MATTER DO IT WITHOUT PASSION

& WITH DISCRETION, HOWEVER

MEAN THE PERSON BE

YOU DO IT TO.

WHEN YOUR SUPERIORS TALK TO ANYBODY HEARKEN NOT,
NEITHER SPEAK NOR LAUGH.

IN COMPANY OF THOSE OF HIGHER QUALITY THAN
YOURSELF, SPEAK NOT TILL YOU ARE ASKED A QUESTION,
THEN STAND UPRIGHT, PUT OFF YOUR HAT & ANSWER
IN FEW WORDS.

· 86th ·

In Disputes, be not So Desirous to Overcome as not
to give Liberty to each one to deliver his Opinion,
and Submit to the judgment of the Major Part
especially if they are Judges of the Dispute.

· 87th ·

Let thy carriage be such as becomes a
Man Grave Settled and attentive to that which is
spoken. Contradict not at every turn what
others Say.

· 88th ·

BE NOT TEDIOUS IN DISCOURSE, MAKE NOT
MANY DIGRESSIONS, NOR REPEAT OFTEN THE SAME
MANNER OF DISCOURSE.

· 89th ·

SPEAK NOT EVIL OF THE ABSENT
FOR IT IS UNJUST.

· 90th ·

BEING SET AT MEAT, SCRATCH NOT, NEITHER SPIT,
COUGH, OR BLOW YOUR NOSE EXCEPT THERE'S
A NECESSITY FOR IT.

MAKE NO SHEW OF TAKING

GREAT DELIGHT IN YOUR VICTUALS,

FEED NOT WITH GREEDINESS; CUT YOUR

BREAD WITH A KNIFE, LEAN NOT

ON THE TABLE, NEITHER FIND FAULT

WITH WHAT YOU EAT.

· 92nd ·

TAKE NO SALT OR
cut BREAD WITH YOUR
KNIFE GREASY.

· 93rd ·

ENTERTAINING ANYONE AT TABLE,
IT IS DECENT TO PRESENT HIM WITH
MEAT. UNDERTAKE NOT TO
HELP OTHERS UNDESIRED
BY THE MASTER.

· 94th ·

IF YOU SOAK BREAD IN THE SAUCE
LET IT BE NO MORE THAN WHAT YOU PUT
IN YOUR MOUTH AT A TIME AND
BLOW NOT YOUR BROTH AT
TABLE BUT STAY TILL IT COOLS
OF ITSELF.

· 95th ·

PUT NOT YOUR MEAT TO YOUR MOUTH
WITH YOUR KNIFE IN YOUR HAND, NEITHER SPIT
FORTH THE STONES OF ANY FRUIT PIE
UPON A DISH, NOR CAST ANYTHING
UNDER THE TABLE.

· 96th ·

IT'S UNBECOMING TO STOOP MUCH TO
ONE'S MEAT. KEEP YOUR FINGERS CLEAN & WHEN
FOUL WIPE THEM ON THE CORNER OF
YOUR TABLE NAPKIN.

· 97th ·

PUT NOT ANOTHER BIT INTO YOUR
MOUTH TILL THE FORMER BE SWALLOWED; LET
NOT YOUR MORSELS BE TOO BIG FOR
THE JOWLS.

· 98th ·

DRINK NOT NOR TALK WITH YOUR
MOUTH FULL, NEITHER GAZE ABOUT YOU
WHILE YOU ARE DRINKING.

· 99th ·

DRINK NOT TOO LEISURELY

NOR YET TOO HASTILY. BEFORE AND

AFTER DRINKING WIPE YOUR LIPS.

BREATHE NOT THEN OR EVER WITH

TOO GREAT A NOISE, FOR

IT'S UNCIVIL.

· 100th ·

CLEANSE NOT YOUR TEETH
WITH THE TABLE CLOTH, NAPKIN, FORK,
OR KNIFE, BUT IF OTHERS DO IT
LET IT BE DONE WITH A
PICK TOOTH.

· 101st ·

RINSE NOT YOUR MOUTH IN THE
PRESENCE OF OTHERS.

· 102nd ·

IT IS OUT OF USE TO CALL UPON
THE COMPANY OFTEN TO EAT, NOR
NEED YOU DRINK TO OTHERS EVERY
TIME YOU DRINK.

· 103rd ·

IN COMPANY OF YOUR BETTERS BE NOT LONGER
IN EATING THAN THEY ARE; LAY NOT YOUR ARM BUT ONLY
YOUR HAND UPON THE TABLE.

· 104th ·

IT BELONGS TO THE CHIEFEST IN COMPANY TO
UNFOLD HIS NAPKIN AND FALL TO MEAT FIRST, BUT HE
OUGHT THEN TO BEGIN IN TIME & TO DISPATCH
WITH DEXTERITY THAT THE SLOWEST MAY
HAVE TIME ALLOWED HIM.

Be not Angry at Table whatever happens & if
you have reason to be so, Shew it not but put on a
Cheerful Countenance especially if there
be Strangers, for Good Humour makes
one Dish of Meat a Feast.

Set not yourself at the upper of the Table
but if it be your Due or that the Master of the
house will have it So, Contend not, least you Should
Trouble the Company.

IF OTHERS TALK AT TABLE BE ATTENTIVE, BUT TALK
NOT WITH MEAT IN YOUR MOUTH.

· 108th ·

WHEN YOU SPEAK OF GOD OR HIS ATTRIBUTES,
LET IT BE SERIOUSLY & WITH REVERENCE. HONOUR & OBEY
YOUR NATURAL PARENTS ALTHOUGH THEY BE POOR.

· 109th ·

LET YOUR RECREATIONS BE MANFUL NOT SINFUL.

L ABOUR TO KEEP ALIVE

IN YOUR BREAST THAT LITTLE

SPARK OF CELESTIAL FIRE

CALLED CONSCIENCE.

FURTHER READING

John Buchanan, *The Road to Valley Forge: How Washington Built the Army that Won the Revolution* (Wiley, 2000)

Bruce Chadwick, *George Washington's War: A Forging of a Revolutionary Leader and American Presidency* (Sourcebooks, 2005)

Joseph J. Ellis, *His Excellency: George Washington* (Knopf, 2004)

David Hackett Fischer, *Washington's Crossing* (Oxford University Press, 2004)

James Thomes Flexner, *Washington: The Indispensable Man* (Back Bay Books, 1994)

Douglas Southall Freeman, *Washington* (Scribner, 1995)

Don Higginbotham (Editor), *George Washington Reconsidered* (University of Virginia Press, 2001)

Robert Leckie, *George Washington's War: The Saga of the American Revolution* (Harper Perennial, 1993)

Edward G. Lengel, *General George Washington: A Military Life* (Random House, 2005)

David McCullough, *1776* (Simon & Schuster, 2005)

William M. S. Rasmussen, Robert S Tilton, *George Washington: the Man Behind the Myths* (University of Virgina Press, 1999)

Henry Wiencek, *An Imperfect God: George Washington, His Slaves and the Creation of America* (Farrar, Straus and Giroux, 2004)